A
BOOK
ABOUT
NAMES

A BOOK

ABOUT NAMES

in which custom, tradition, law, myth,
history, folklore, foolery, legend, fashion,
nonsense, symbol, taboo help explain how
we got our names and what they mean

by Milton Meltzer
drawings by Mischa Richter

Thomas Y. Crowell   New York

Excerpt on page 46 from "Mary's a Grand Old Name" (George M. Cohan)
Copyright © GEORGE M. COHAN MUSIC PUBLISHING COMPANY. Used
by permission.

A Book about Names

Text copyright © 1984 by Milton Meltzer
Illustrations copyright © 1984 by Mischa Richter

Library of Congress Cataloging in Publication Data
Meltzer, Milton, date
    A book about names.
    Summary: Offers tidbits from history, folklore,
tradition, and other sources that help explain how
people got their names and what they mean.
    1. Names, Personal—Juvenile literature.   2. Names,
Personal—Folklore—Juvenile literature.   3. Nicknames—
Juvenile literature.   [1. Names, Personal. 2. Nicknames]
I. Richter, Mischa, date, ill. II. Title.
CS2305.M44 1984   929.4   83-45241
ISBN 0-690-04380-5
ISBN 0-690-04381-3 (lib. bdg.)

Designed by Al Cetta

1 2 3 4 5 6 7 8 9 10

First Edition

FOREWORD

*"Must a name mean something?" Alice asked doubtfully.
"Of course it must," Humpty Dumpty said. . . . "My name
means the shape I am. . . . With a name like yours, you
might be any shape, almost."*

Names are symbols. So are most other words. But what
names symbolize is unique. A hundred other people may
have borne your name, but none of them was just like you.
Who else could have had your past, your hopes, your fears,
your joys, your sorrows? So the name you carry means
something special, something particular, something that
is *you*. It makes you aware of yourself as somebody different from everyone else. A name—your name—is a symbol more powerful than any other word.

Whatever your given name, it has a cultural meaning
that affects the image other people form of you as the bearer
of that name. How you feel about your own name may

shape your personality in a positive or negative way. Your parents, or whoever named you, revealed the nature of their interests and concerns and the frame of their culture by their choice of the name they gave you.

There has long been a widespread belief in the power of names. When a name changes, some say, the person changes. Take the true story of Saul Kurzweil. He was a child in Eastern Europe when an epidemic struck his village and he fell seriously ill. To deceive the Angel of Death, Saul's mother carried him to the synagogue and there had her son renamed Chaim, meaning "life." It fooled the Angel, and Saul recovered.

On the other hand, some thought sickness could be caused by a name. Among certain American Indians and the people of Tibet it was believed that names that did not fit the person could bring on illness. The cure was to take a new name that would fit better. And in ancient times Chinese doctors would write a patient's name on a piece of paper, then burn the paper and mix the ashes with medicine to guarantee that the medicine would cure the sick person.

Inseparable from a name's meaning and power is its sound. "You can love a name," said Gertrude Stein, "and if you love a name, then saying that name any number of times can only make you love it more." Poetry, she added, is "really loving the name of anything."

The study of names (the scholars call it onomastics) has produced a considerable bibliography, which I have freely and gratefully drawn upon. The references venture into history, psychology, anthropology, sociology, linguistics. The many paths into the realm of names and naming are worth pursuing. But what follows is a sample for the casual reader of the pleasures to be found in what the serious students have unearthed.

This is a book written for the fun of it. The reader can

begin at the beginning and go straight on to the end. Or just take quick bites, here, there or anywhere. While it's not a "serious" book, many items, I hope, offer insights into history and human relationships.

For readers who have an interest in a particular subject area, the index will prove a helpful guide.

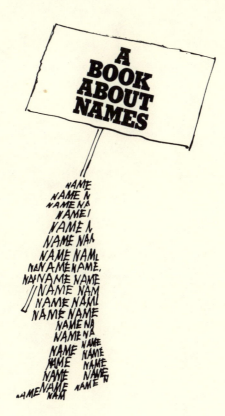

CRAZY-ROUND-BEAVER

All kinds of pigeonholes can be found into which names are slotted. Often these categories are rigidly fixed, and every name must be fitted into them. The Seminole Indians draw on three elements for their names and combine all three without any regard for their meanings. They have a "moral" series of names, which would seem to refer to character or temperament: cautious, crazy, wise, malicious, et cetera. Then there is a series having to do with shapes: round, square, elongated, etc. And finally a "zoological" or animal series: eagle, beaver, wolf, puma, etc. They take a term from each series and, putting them together, come up with a name like Crazy-Round-Beaver.

Something Fishy

You can amuse yourself by picking any odd category of names and seeing how many examples you can find in your phone book. Take fish: I cast a line into the Manhattan directory and hooked a Bass, a Pike, an Oyster, a Goldfisch, a Haddock. But to go beyond today's directory: other fish too have given their names to people of greater or lesser distinction. There is Margaret *Whiting*, George *Crabbe*, Hubert *Herring*, Robert *Trout*, Louise *Mullet*, Patricia *Pickrel*, Jack *Sharkey*, James *Whale*, Jarold *Sole*, Birdie *Salmon*, to name a few. And Hamilton *Fish* itself is a grand old name that has decorated the halls of Congress for generations.

FIRST FAMILY

No one knows when the first family names, or surnames, originated or began to be passed on down the generations. Among different peoples and cultures, naming followed varying patterns. Family names among the Chinese go back to the fourth century B.C. and perhaps even earlier among the Hindus. In the West, the ancient Romans developed an elaborate system of naming that changed over the long centuries of the Republic and the Empire.

Honor among Anglo-Saxons

Back in Old England, the Anglo-Saxons used only what we call a first name, and they had an enormous variety of them. A name was a man's property, honoring him and kept for him alone. No sons could be named after him. It meant that new names had constantly to be invented. Often such names were created to express ideas—of courage, cunning, power, brightness. Such a name, they believed, would then endow the newborn with that quality.

14

They Just Grew

In England, there were no hereditary family names much before the Norman Conquest of 1066. It took about a hundred years after the Conquest for family names to develop. They rose up spontaneously; no one laid down the law on names. They simply grew out of everyday speech because they were needed. Most came from the farming and working people, echoing their lively voices and rough talk. Scholars estimate there are about 100,000 current surnames of British origin. They tell us much about what people were saying and doing when that casual naming of neighbors took hold.

To Tell One John from Another

Surnames came out of the need to tell one person from another. Suppose there was one John in the village and then another showed up. People needed a way to indicate which John they were talking about. So they began to say John the Red (because of the color of his hair), or John Little (because he was small), or John the Proud, or John the Miller, or John of the Woods. Nicknames, these were, and a very common source of surnames. Temporary at first, they were not passed on to the next generation. Slowly, however, these nicknames, or second names, shifted into permanent family names. And with the Norman Conquest they became widespread. By 1300, it was the usual thing to have two names. More, it was necessary for those rare times when your identity had to be put down in writing. A man didn't want to have to pay taxes twice because he was confused with someone else. So he signed his name in full on the tax rolls.

THE FOUR TYPES

Most Europeon surnames or family names fall into four types. Originally, they referred to (1) a locality, (2) a relationship, (3) an occupation, or (4) a description or characteristic of the person named. An example of #1 is Abraham *Lincoln*, for a town in England. #2: Samuel *Johnson*, for the son of John. #3: Elizabeth *Taylor*, for the occupation of a tailor. (Tailor could be Portnoy in Russian, Schneider in German, Kravitz in Polish or Ukrainian, Sherman in Yiddish, Chait in Hebrew.) #4: Charles *Beard*, for the chin whiskers of his ancestor.

SHORT AND STOUT

Names of personal description—suggested by the way a person looked or acted—are abundant. Thomas *Hardy*, Bobby *Short*, Rex *Stout*, Henry Wadsworth *Longfellow*, Hugo *Black*, John *Bright*, Louis *Armstrong*, Oscar *Wilde*, Helen Wills *Moody*, Stephen *Wise*, Andrew *Young*, E. B. *White*, Jonathan *Swift*, Ronald *Blythe*.

18

Fields and Rivers

The landscape, any particular part of it, has been a rich source of names. Here's just a scattering of them: Ethel *Waters*, Sam *Moore*, Grant *Wood*, Reginald *Marsh*, Alexander *Brook*, Henry *Ford*, H. G. *Wells*, Ernest *Poole*, Veronica *Lake*, George *Grove*, Leon *Meadow*, Joseph *Fields*, Henry *Green*, E. D. *Rivers*, Priscilla *Lane*, James J. *Hill*, Nathaniel *Banks*.

Back in the days when feudal lords could afford legions of household retainers, the functions they performed became the root of their names. Such names have come down through the centuries to us, no longer statements of fact. There's Neville *Chamberlain*, John *Butler*, Charlie *Chaplin* (for chaplain, who says grace), Samuel *Barber*, Andrew *Porter*, Hilda *Bailey* (for bailiff), Austin *Stewart*, Jack *Warden*, Christopher *Reeve*, William *Page*, Jimmy *Carter*, Maureen *Forester*, Donald *Saddler*.

Deacon and Priest

Some medieval surnames reflected the social standing or office held by their owners: Anthony *Burgess*, Eric *Knight*, Orville *Freeman*, John *Constable*, Jose-Luis *Clerc*, J. C. *Squire*, Charles *Baron*, George *Abbott*, Philip *Deacon*, Alexander *Pope*, Joseph *Priestley*, Clarence *King*, Claudia *Cardinale*.

Fiddle-dee-dee

Medieval life wasn't all fighting or praying or laboring in the fields. People had fun, too, and those who provided the entertainment took appropriate names. These names survive in: Arthur *Fiedler*, Norton *Juster* (for jester), Ida Usted *Harper*, Douglas *Player*.

BUILDERS

The building trades are, of course, indispensable at any time in history. The artisans who put up houses and churches and palaces acquired the names of their trade, and now we recognize them in Richard *Wright* (workman), George *Mason*, Tom *Sawyer*, Clifford *Carpenter*, Anne *Tyler* (tile layer), Christopher *Plummer* (a worker in lead), Margaret *Thatcher*, George *Painter*.

The Most Common

Three surnames are almost always the most common in any directory you pick up in the English-speaking world. They are Smith, Clark, and Taylor—all occupational names. The first supplied weapons and tools; the second, a little learning; and the third, clothing. Close upon their heels come Miller and Baker, suppliers of food. Although the vast majority of occupational names have come down as surnames, occasionally they are used as first names: Wright Morris (a wright in Middle English meant worker or maker) and Hunter Thompson.

hello, Joe!

In conversation, people were called by their first names (though they may have had two names) up through medieval times. Not long before Columbus sailed on his first voyage, this custom began to change. And rapidly, as did almost everything else at the beginning of the modern era. For the next four hundred years or so, people were addressed formally, by their surname. That is, except in the intimate circle of family or friends. Not until our time, the twentieth century, did the use of the first name become common again in conversation.

ELEGANCE

By the time Chaucer was born, the great mass of English surnames was firmly set. About two hundred and fifty years later, in Shakespeare's day, the aristocrats did an about-face and turned surnames into first names. By the nineteenth century, the middle class was imitating the people who set fashion. They gave their children first names borrowed from the aristocratic surnames of the great dukes and earls and lords: Percy, Sidney, Neville, Russell, Howard. There was no family connection, but it sounded elegant. The custom became even more popular in America.

ROYAL FLUSH

JOHN AND MARY LIVE HERE

British royalty set the model for popular first names, often turned later into surnames. Henry, Edward, John, Elizabeth, Mary, Charles, William, Alfred, Richard, Victoria, and Anne gave their names to innumerable children throughout the Empire—luckily, without the nickname that often followed: the Bold, the Simple, the Fat . . .

What Puritans Prefer

The Puritans, who settled in early New England, felt that they were the true heirs of the Old Testament; trying to mark their children off from the "godless masses," they invented many strange names for them. One Puritan minister called his children Much-mercy, Increased, Sin-deny, and Fear-not. Another named a child Safe-on-high. Matching these for oddity were Free-gift, Dust, Ashes, Obedience, More-trial, Discipline, Praise-God, and Live-well. Infants found after their parents had abandoned them inspired Puritan ministers to creative heights. The innocent foundlings were tagged for life with such names as Helpless, Repentance, Lament, Forsaken, Flie-fornication, and even Misericordia-adulterina.

IN AFRICA

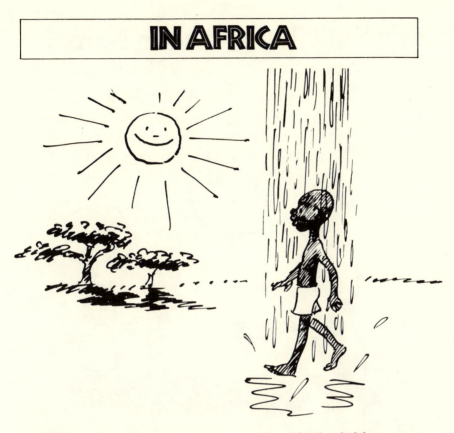

In Africa, the naming ceremonies for black children are fairly consistent throughout the continent. Taken into consideration are the time of day the child is born, the day of the week, and, frequently, special circumstances linked to the child, its parents, its extended family, and the community. To show their happiness at the birth, parents often give names meaning "rejoice," "we are blessed," "luck," "gift of God." Some African names, such as Rain, reflect what happened at the time of birth. Not until the child has been named is it considered a person (perhaps because of the high infant mortality in some places). The final naming is thus seen to complete the act of birth. Many Africans believe it is only the body that dies; the spirit lives on, dwelling in many bodies in many lifetimes.

So You Changed Your Name?

Most African names are single words or a few words shaped into a phrase in the language of the family. For instance, the Yoruba male and female name Ayo means "joy," while the girl's name Ayodele means "joy enters the home." But beyond that first given name, Africans adopt or are given other names, too, so that someone you knew by a particular name some years ago might have an altogether different name when you meet him today. The advertisements in African newspapers frequently carry announcements of people who have changed their personal names or their surnames. Children born of the same parents may have quite different names, because in many African societies family names do not exist.

AMERICAN NAMES?

What is an American name? There is no such thing—except, of course, for Native American names. In a nation of immigrants, everyone has come bearing a name from another culture. As the mixture has grown richer, so has the variety of names. And all, in this sense, are foreign. Americans bear the names of peoples of all colors, creeds, and classes, from every continent on earth.

Original unto Death

The Jews—and many other peoples, too—believed names affect the persons who carry them, like taboos or charms. Treatises by Jewish sages take up these matters in considerable detail. Orthodox Jews traditionally named their children after worthy forebears. Ignoring fashion, they preserved the same names generation after generation. But the first American-born generation of Jews after the great immigration from Eastern Europe that began in the 1880s turned from that path. No longer did they name grandchildren after an esteemed Isaac. Instead, the name became Ernest, Edward, Edmund, Eric; not Nathan, but Norman or Norton or Newton. Moses blossomed out as Maurice, Morris, Morton, Murray. Nevertheless, most Jews still bear their "original" Jewish name, and this name, in Hebrew or Yiddish, is the one pronounced by the rabbi when they are lowered into the grave.

PROTECTIVE COLORATION

The rejection of traditional Biblical names was not unique to American Jews. Jews everywhere adopted Aramaic, Greek, Anglo-Saxon, French, Italian, German, or Slavic names when they dwelt among those nations. The assimilation of foreign names—for protective coloration?—goes way back to Babylonian days. These adopted names became so commonplace among Jews in whatever country Jews inhabited that after a time, ironically, the very names they had taken were looked upon by the Gentiles as typically Jewish names. The fashion for certain Gentile names among Jews inevitably led Gentiles to shy away from those names. Thus, in Germany, Moritz concealed Moses for many decades, until Jews realized that Gentiles had dropped Moritz. It happened in England and in America, too.

Trouble Entering Paradise

Whatever countries immigrants came from (unless it was Britain), their difficult names gave the officials at Castle Garden or Ellis Island a headache. Not bothering to get the newcomers' names right, they put down something roughly like what they heard, or wrote a totally different name on the bewildered immigrant's entry record. When the children started school, the teachers found some of their surnames unpronounceable and entered on the rolls something close enough but easier to say. After a time the parents themselves would adopt the new names the children brought home.

The Czar's Fancy

It was Czar Alexander I who, in 1804, forced the Jews of Russia to acquire surnames. Up to then the Jews of Eastern Europe had generally been known by their personal names, plus their father's name, as in Yaakov ben Yitzhak (ben means "son of"). Fixed family names would help the government in levying taxes and conscripting Jewish soldiers. The Czar also hoped it would push the Jews toward assimilating. For the bureaucrats in charge of granting and registering names, it was still another chance to extort money from Jews. Handsome names—like Diamant and Saphir (for jewels) or Rosenthal and Lilienthal (for flowers)—came high. Those unable to afford such names were stuck with ugly ones, like Schmaltz, Lumpe, Schmuck, Rundskopf, Eselkopf, Fresser, Wantz.

Where Jews could escape the authorities, they sometimes invented brand-new names, or took them from literature or from the priestly caste, or turned Hebrew or Yiddish first names into surnames, or created a patronym. In Slavic countries patronyms were made by adding the suffixes -vitch, -ov, -eff, -off, and -kin to denote "descendant of"—hence Abramovitch for descendant of Abram; Aronoff, for Aaron; Rivkin, for Rivke. Among Austrian and German Jews this was done with the suffix -sohn: thus Mendelsohn or Isaacsohn.

THE WHEEL TURNS

There is a cyclical pattern in the behavior of immigrant generations. And it affects names and naming as much as anything else. Sociologists find that the children of immigrants usually tend to reject the forms of their parents' ethnic behavior. The children try to fit into the new setting by getting rid of everything that seems "foreign" and "strange." It is a way of seeking quick acceptance. *Their* children, however—the third generation in the new land—tend to feel quite at home as Americans. They don't worry so much about the culture and religion of their grandparents. Often they take a fresh look at them and adopt what they have come to cherish. So the third generation of Jews in America, for example, has often turned to the Old Testament for names to give their children. And back come Abraham, Aaron, Asa, Amos, Joseph, David, Esther, Leah, Gideon, Miriam, Sarah, Hannah. As one scholar put it, what the sons of immigrants wish to forget, the grandchildren wish to remember.

"Too Foreign"

It wasn't only a natural desire "to be American" like everybody else that accounts for changes in immigrant names. Many firms refused to hire people whose names ended in something sounding Jewish or Greek or Polish or Italian. That was "too foreign" for their patrons was the excuse. If the elite would not trade with or hire people with certain names, then the names were changed. The old folks, especially, minded such loss of a family name. But if being stubborn meant to starve?

Pen Name

At the age of twenty-seven, Samuel L. Clemens, a reporter, signed a newspaper story "Mark Twain." He was inventing a new name for himself as he dropped out of journalism and into literature. He was but one of many writers who chose another name for their writing self. In the nineteenth century, women novelists took men's names because their times discouraged them from publishing under their own names. Take the Brontë sisters: Charlotte wrote as Currer Bell, Anne as Acton Bell, and Emily as Ellis Bell, though their real names now appear on their works. Mary Ann Evans's novels came out in the name of George Eliot, and they still do. In France, Amandine Aurore Lucie Dupin published as George Sand.

For very different reasons, Cicily Fairfield chose to replace that genteel name with Rebecca West, the brilliant and rebellious heroine created by the playwright Ibsen. You can make a game of matching pen name to author: Lewis Carroll was Charles Lutwidge Dodgson; Sholem Aleichem: Solomon Rabinowitz; George Orwell: Eric Blair; O. Henry: William Sydney Porter; Boz: Charles Dickens; Geoffrey Crayon: Washington Irving.

Dzhugashvili?

The assuming of new names by political rebels is common. Nikolai Lenin did it, and so did Leon Trotsky and Joseph Stalin. The real names of these Soviet leaders were Vladimir Ilich Ulyanov, Lev Davidovich Bronstein, and Iosif Vissarionovich Dzhugashvili. When they dropped their own names and chose new ones, it symbolized a deep change in their lives. It also helped them throw the police off their tracks.

EL CHE

ERNESTO GUEVARA

Some famous people have acquired more than one nickname in a lifetime. Take Ernesto Guevara, the legendary guerrilla fighter. As a youngster he was called El Chancho, meaning "the slob." When he became a revolutionary, his followers called him El Che, or Buddy. Shortly before he was captured and killed in Bolivia, he said that the most important and cherished part of his life was Che, his new name. "Everything that came before it," he said, "my surname and my Christian names, are minor, personal, and insignificant details."

BORN ON WEDNESDAY

Names can have a powerful effect upon personal behavior. A study of the Ashanti people of West Africa illustrates the point. The Ashanti name their children according to the day of the week on which they are born. Monday boys, it is widely believed, are quiet and well-behaved, but Wednesday boys are said to be hot-tempered and aggressive. Reports on the behavior of Ashanti children revealed that Monday boys were indeed less frequently delinquent than chance would have it, while Wednesday boys were more often guilty of attacks upon people. The conclusion: there is a tendency for Ashanti boys to live up to their names.

SMITHOLOGY

It takes a Smith to estimate the number of Smiths this world contains. And this unique Smith (Elsdon C.) figures there are over 2.2 million Smiths alive in the United States. That is one Smith for every one hundred Americans. If the estimator, an eminent names specialist, included all the variants—Smyth, Smythe, Smits, Schmidt, et cetera—then we could add a hundred thousand more. The figures are based on machine counts of Social Security records. With Smith so common a name, parents seeking distinction for their offspring have favored such first names as Five-Eighths (5/8) Smith and Loyal Lodge No. 296 Knights of Pythias Ponca City Oklahoma Smith and even Christ Smith. Despite the frequency of Smiths, none has ever been elected President of the United States, although one ran. But several Smiths have earned fame. Which one was a pioneer economist? A sculptor? A Marine commandant? A signer of the Declaration of Independence? A Western explorer? A humorist? A World War II general? A dime novelist? A Biblical scholar? A philanthropist? An inventor of the typewriter? Of sticky flypaper? Of a revolver? Who was the first woman to be elected to the US Senate in her own right? Which one founded the Mormon Church? Stitched the first pair of bloomers?

Take My Hammer

Why is Smith the most common surname of them all? The vast majority of these Smiths take their name from an ancestor's trade. The term originally meant any craftsman using a hammer, and it included workers in metal, wood, and stone. But why should Smith as a surname outweigh all other names derived from occupations? Was the smith so important a force in his community? Or was it that in medieval England, when surnames were taken on, long periods of war demanded many smiths to shape the weapons? Whatever the case, Smiths became common names in the languages of many countries: in German, Schmidt; in Czech, Kovar; in Italian, Ferrari; in Spanish, Herrera; in Polish, Kowalski; in Finnish, Seppanen; in Syrian, Hadad.

GOING BY THE RULES

Should names be regulated in any way? In England the law does not require you to have a name. The Germans determine which names can be used and which cannot, and insist that a name entered in the official record must be kept for life. They also oblige a wife to take her husband's name on marriage. The Anglican Church insists that a child be named, and the Roman Catholic Church requires that a baby be given a saint's name. At confirmation, Christians have a second chance to acquire a new name, and it is then that Roman Catholics often add another saint to their name.

Name Collector

A European beauty was celebrated for collecting famous husbands. As she went from one marriage to the next, she refused to drop the name of the previous husbands. She ended up known as Alma Mahler Gropius Werfel. Gustav Mahler was a composer-conductor, Walter Gropius was an architect, and Franz Werfel a novelist.

Jennifer, Jennifer, Jennifer

MARY

> But it was Mary, Mary,
> Long before the fashions came,
> And there is something there,
> That sounds so fair,
> It's a grand old name.

Yes, it was simple and plain and ever so popular, as George M. Cohan's lyrics proclaim. But Mary is no longer among the ten most popular girls' names registered in New York. During the 1970s Jennifer was at the top, followed by Jessica, Melissa, Nicole, Michelle, Elizabeth, Lisa, Tiffany, Christina, and Danielle. Maybe now people want to be different.

STARS IN THEIR EYES

The movies have long had a strong influence on the choice of names. With the rise of each star, thousands of parents in the 30s, 40s, and 50s hoped for reflected glory in naming their babies Shirley (Temple), Gary (Cooper), Carole (Lombard), Joan (Crawford), Leslie (Caron), Linda (Darnell), Maureen (O'Sullivan), Marlene (Dietrich), Myrna (Loy), Merle (Oberon). In many cases, such names were themselves the fanciful invention of performers shedding ordinary or ethnic names. Often such names were imposed upon the stars by studio executives who feared the public would not accept actors from Italian, Jewish, or other ethnic minority groups. No longer true, of course, as John Travolta, George Segal, Barbra Streisand, Al Pacino, and Robert de Niro testify. Streisand went even further, refusing to bob her nose.

CELEBRITIES

ALEXANDER

The craze for celebrities goes back a long way and has always influenced the giving of names. When Alexander the Great swept across continents and reached Palestine in 333 B.C., he permitted limited self-rule for the Jews. Countless Jews thereafter named sons after him, sometimes shortening Alexander to Sender. In England, Hugh of Lincoln, a church martyr of the thirteenth century, made the name Hugh immensely popular. Babies born in the month of March are often named after Saint Patrick. Ardent Zionists have named their sons Theodore Herzl after Theodor Herzl, the founder of the modern Zionist movement.

A SHORTAGE OF NAMES

The naming customs of some societies consume so many names that shortages are threatened. Take the Tiwi people of the Melville and Bathurst islands of North Australia. In their system of allotting proper names, the children are given special names according to the stages of their development. As a male goes from his fifteenth to twenty-sixth year, he uses up seven names. Women use up seven from their tenth to twenty-first years. Each person has an average of three names, and all these names have to be unique. No other person can carry the same name. Upon a person's death, there is not only a ban on the reuse of all the names he has borne, but also on those names that he may have given to others, whether his own or someone else's children, during the course of his life. When a woman remarries, her husband gives new names to all the children she already has. The way this works out, no Tiwi can be sure that he or she will keep a name for good until the mother dies.

Vegetable Kingdom

Nature's vegetable substances have provided us with many names. Phillis *Wheatley*, the poet; Joyce Carol *Oates*, the novelist; Bertram *Korn*, the historian; Elmer *Rice*, the playwright. And long ago, the people who supplied food took on the names of their occupations: Fisher, of course, and Baker, Miller, Fowler, Hunter, Shepherd . . .

Jolly Saint Nick

Saints' names began to flourish in the fourth century in England, Italy, and Germany. Even those of quite obscure saints. (Friends of mine named their daughters after three of them: Felicitas, Dorcas, and Crispina.) Saint Mary and Saint John lead all the rest in popularity. The saint who delights children at Christmastime, Nicholas, was a bishop in Asia Minor who lived at about the end of the third century. Known to be kind and gentle, he was said to creep up to windows during the night to fling in gold dowries for poor girls who needed them in order to marry. His name comes down to us in several forms: Nicol, Nicholson, Nickles, Nix, Nixon.

Poets who made their own names famous never expected that in generations to come those names would be tacked on to innocent babes by ambitious parents: *Shelley* Winters, *Keats* Speed, *Coleridge* Taylor Perkinson, *Byron* Garson, and, alas, *Milton* Meltzer.

Stark, the Pussycat

The way a person looked or behaved gave rise to many nicknames: Big, Little, Stout, Old, Shorter, Elder, Strong, Ambler, Trotter. Once given, the nickname was hard to shake off. It might pass down in the family, turning into a surname. One or two generations later, there was probably no connection between the appearance of a descendant and the name he bore. Mr. Strong might be puny, Mr. Swift a slowpoke, Mr. Bright a dullard, Mr. Stark (which once meant "fierce" or "savage"), a pussycat.

E. T. McGee

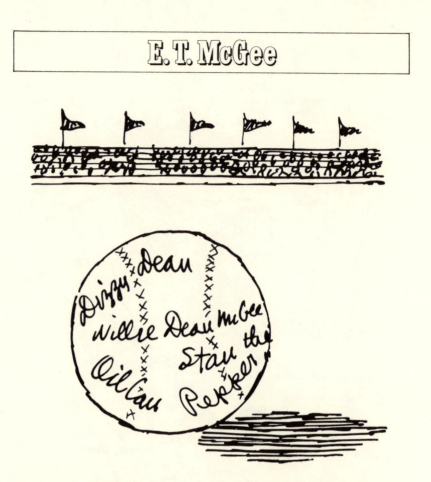

Nicknames? Baseball history sparkles with them. The St. Louis Cardinals for the last half-century boasted some of the most popular ones: Dizzy Dean, Pepper Martin, Stan the Man Musial, Harry the Cat Breecheen, Whitey Kurowki, Country Slaughter. But "E. T." McGee? No thank you, said the star rookie of the 1982 World Series. A young center-fielder no one had heard of before, he hit two home runs for a Cardinal victory. The astonished fans thought he had landed in the World Series directly from another planet. So "E. T." was what they began calling him. "Don't call me that," said Willie Dean McGee. "Nobody should be able to change your name. It's almost like changing your life."

FATSO

"Fatso," "Skinny," "Shorty," "Stretch"—nicknames all, and familiar to every kid on the block. But kings, too, were stuck with nicknames. William I was tagged either the Conqueror or the Bastard. William II was Rufus (the red-haired). Richard I was called the Lion-Hearted. Edward I—unusual in his day for his six feet two inches—was Longshanks. Richard III was Crouchback. The subjects of those kings labored under harsher nicknames. London records show men called Stunch (smell), Wigga (beetle), Holobuc (hollow belly), Hore (filth), and Forfoot (big feet). Thousands of years before those English kings and commoners, people in ancient Egypt called each other by such sorry nicknames as Ape, Mouse, Baldy, Lazy, Big Head. No matter where or when, people have had similar tastes in nicknames.

Mr. Q

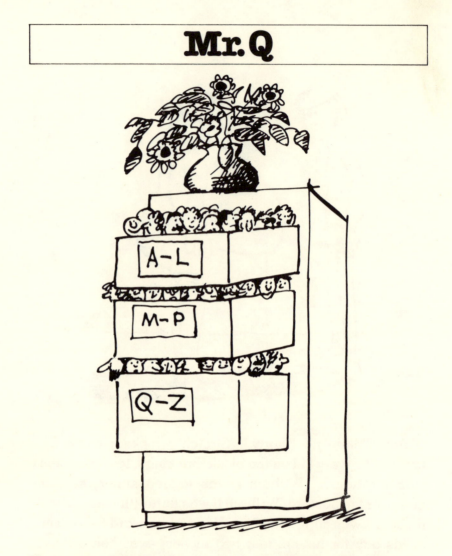

How many *different* surnames are there? One clue to quantity is found in a recent register of the U.S. Social Security Administration. It listed nearly 1.3 million different family names. And more than one-third of these occurred only once. Some Americans are so unusual that they use just a single letter for a name—Q or X or Z or A. You'll find just about every letter of the alphabet standing for someone's family name.

In Japan

The Japanese did not all take surnames until commanded to do so by the Emperor Meiji in the nineteenth century. They often put together two words to make a surname. One or both of them may refer to a place in nature. Tanaka is *Ta*, ricefield, and *naka*, middle. Hayakawa combines *haya*, early and *kawa*, river. Fujikawa links wisteria to river, and Kawasaki, river to headland.

Back to the Roots

One of the most widely publicized persons in the world in recent times has been Muhammad Ali, long the world champion heavyweight boxer. A universally respected athlete, he became a folk hero. His given name was Cassius Clay (itself the name of a white Kentuckian who fought against slavery in his home territory). The modern Cassius Clay took his new name in the 1960s, influenced by the Black Muslim movement. The Muslims were saying that we are what we are without reference to what the slave masters of another time named us. Many of the new names taken by Muslims come from African languages. This was "going back to the roots," something black parents wished to express when they gave a child an African name.

One, Two, Three

The same customs for naming children pop up in many parts of the world. Parents may choose names to show the order in which the holder of the name was born. The Romans used the Latin Una for One; Secundus for Second, Quintus for Fifth, Octavian for Eighth, and so on. The Spanish dubbed the firstborn son Primo. In Japan, babies often have numbers for their names: Ichiko means "Number One Child," or firstborn. In Michigan, a family by the name of Stickney named their sons One, Two, Three Stickney, their daughters First, Second, and Third Stickney. The Ashanti in West Africa sometimes used a similar system.

COME THE REVOLUTION

Strange names were given to Russian babies after the Revolution of 1917. Instead of the common Ivan or Boris, children were saddled with such names as Utopiya or Ninel (for Lenin spelled backwards). Science and technology plus communism would remake the world, the Russians thought, so babies were burdened with such names as Radi for radium and Gali for helium, or were even called Traktor or Elektrifikataiya. Two ambitious parents who expected their child to do great things named him Genii (Genius). By the 1940s that fad faded, and now Aleksandr and Sergei are among the most popular male names in Russia.

Inability to spell accurately gave rise to more mutations in names than Mendel induced in his peas. Changing fashions in spelling have also played a part in such variations. In Shakespeare's time his name was spelled in eighty-three different ways. Even American Presidents, whose names now seem permanently carved in stone, have not been immune from change. George Washington's half brother, Lawrence, was known as Wasshington when a student at Oxford. Jefferson was once Jeffeson and Giffersonne. The changes rung on Jackson included Jakson, Jacson, Jackeson, Jakeson, and Jaxon. Lincoln suffered through Lincolne, Lyncoln, Lincon, and Linkhorn. What fixed the names permanently was the spread of education and the use of dictionaries.

Strange and Unearthly

"Strange and unearthly" surnames do pop up even in our own time. Take Miss Dagmar Sewer or Miss Mary Lou Wham. A life-insurance company once amused the public with a list of colorful names borne by its policy-holders. Among these were Oscar Apathy, Julia Barefoot, Barnum Bobo, John Bilious, Alphonse Forgetto, Ansen Outhouse, and Chintz Royalty.

Bob and Ted and Dan and Jimmy

Fashions in names come and go, just like politicians. Not long ago, most congressmen paraded their full names—the longer, the more prestigious-sounding: listen to the drumbeat of Rogers Clark Ballard Morton, senator from Maryland. Or they favored using a first initial and middle name: F. Bradford Morse, Republican of Massachusetts. But now, about one out of six members of Congress have adopted nicknames for *official* use. Senator Robert William Packwood is known as Bob Packwood. Congressman Daniel David Rostenkowski is just plain Dan. Senator Theodore F. Stevens of Alaska is simply Ted. Even James Earl Carter, Jr., demanded to be known as President Jimmy Carter. A few politicians always had informal names, among them President Harry S Truman and Speaker of the House Sam Rayburn. But these two men were baptized as such.

THE "REAL" NAME?

In our society only men have "real" names, say the feminists. The man's name is permanent; the woman gives up her name in marriage. It is the man's name that is given to the children. The woman's family name doesn't count. She loses her identity. So history becomes the story of the male line. Try to document what women have done and see how hard it is to trace them in the sources; because their names change, they seem to disappear.

Stop a moment and think how odd it is that we say women "marry into" a family and that if a family produces no sons the family is said to "die out." No wonder a majority of parents polled say they would rather have a son than a daughter as a first or only child. They see family and name as one and the same, with the male the carrier of its history. How arbitrary is a definition of "family" that cuts out the female line of descent!

Whose Name at Marriage?

Does the newlywed wife have to take her husband's name?
Few women realize that it's only a tradition. In America no
law compels them to do it. (Up until 1975 Hawaii did have
such a law, although it was never enforced.) They have a
right to keep their original name, and in recent years many
more wives have gone under their own names, or with a
hyphen adding their husband's name to theirs. The grow-
ing number of women entering careers often wish to keep
their name, the name they established by their own efforts
in a business or profession.

Cohen and Levy

EN YCOHEN LEVY COHEN LEVYCOHENLEVY COHEN LEVYCOH EN LEVY COHENLEVYCOHEN LEVY COHEN LEVY COHEN COHENLEVYCOHENLEVYCOHEN Y COHENLEVYCOHENLEVYCOHEN Y COHEN LEVY COHEN LE VY COHEN LEVY COHEN LE VY CO HEN LEV Y COHEN

Cohen is the most common Jewish surname in the United States, in New York City surpassing even Smith. A Hebrew word, Cohen originally meant "a prince" or "a priest," but later it came to mean "a priest" only. In Jewish tradition, the name was confined to descendants of Aaron, first high priest and brother of Moses, but that tradition faded away. Now the name has many variants, such as Cohn, Cone, Cowan, Cohan, Coen, Kohn, and Kohen. (Cohan and Coen are Irish names, too.) Levy, like Cohen, has many variants. The name comes from the tribe of Levites, in biblical times, who were assigned to the care of the Ark and the Tabernacle and later of the Temple. From the original Hebrew name of Levi have come Levi, Levy, Lewy, Levey, Levin, Levine, Levitan, Lewisohn, Lewis, Lever, Lee, and Leeds.

THE NAME-GIVER

The ancient tribal tradition of the Delaware Indians of Oklahoma bestowed the function of name-giving on those individuals blessed with visions inspired by the Creator. The visionaries were gifted people with powers ordinary people did not have. They were able to give names to their own children and the children of others. Those who were not gifted with visions—the great majority—could confer nicknames on their children, but not real names. Such nicknames were used in everyday exchanges among tribal members. But the real personal name was the mark of identity by which the Creator and his Spirit Forces knew the individual. Some Delawares would never reveal their real name beyond the immediate family. In the hands of one capable of conjuring evil, a person's real name might do him harm, causing disability, blindness, and even death. Such sorcery or witchcraft could not happen with a nickname. The name-giver did not name a newly born baby. The parents would wait until they were reasonably sure the Creator meant the child to remain permanently in the family. Meanwhile, the baby went by a nickname, and at the right time, got the real name from a visionary.

Great Jumpin' Jehoshaphat!

A popular music hall song of the 1870s amused audiences with a recital of the problems caused the performer by his extraordinarily long name. When he came to the chorus, with a faintly Irish lilt, he would reel off his burden:

> Jonathan, Joseph, Jeremiah,
> Timothy, Titus, Obadiah,
> William, Henry, Walter, Sim,
> Reuben, Rufus, Solomon, Jim,
> Nathaniel, Daniel, Abraham,
> Roderick, Frederick, Peter, Sam,
> Simon, Dimon, Nicholas, Pat,
> Christopher, Dick, Jehoshaphat.

WHO'S REALLY WHO?

If you came across a list of such names as Addition, Crook, Damp, Jump, Moose, Needy, Outlaw, Stretch, and Vest you might guess they were culled from the novels of Charles Dickens. But no, these are real names, and they all come from one edition of *Who's Who*. These people didn't break into that august directory because of their odd names, but for having distinguished themselves in other ways. The same edition lists Bellow, Dingle, Dowdy, Gasser, Jeeves, Looney, Nepple, Noggle, Oddy, Peachey, Reckless, Sizoo, Swindler, Tingle, Tippy, Tuggle, and Twitty. The scholar Elsdon C. Smith, who unearthed these gems, reasons that "the taunts and insults they must have endured in school by reason of their names . . . must have spurred them on to success."

69

Hitler's Choice

In the Germany of the 1930s, Hitler used name laws as a weapon against the Jews. The Nazi goal was to convince the German people that the Jews in their midst were the enemy and had to be put down. Hitler issued name decrees designed to identify Jews and thereby set them apart from the mass of Germans with whom they shared the same language, customs, occupations, and names. If a Jew did not already have one of the acceptable "Jewish" names selected from the Old Testament by the Nazis, the male was required to add Israel to his given names and the female to add Sarah. This additional name was thereafter to be used with the signature on every official document and communication. The intent was to degrade Jews in the eyes of fellow Germans and to make easier the other steps setting Jews apart: the Star of David affixed to clothing, the red "J" stamped on passports, the "*Jude*" marked on ration books. By a person's "Jewish" name his identity as an inferior creature would be known. It was an early push down the slope to extinction.

I'M NOBODY

I'm Nobody! Who are you?
Are you—Nobody—too?
Then there's a pair of us!
Don't tell! they'd banish us—you know!
How dreary—to be—Somebody!
How public—like a Frog—
To tell your name—the livelong June—
To an admiring Bog!

                         Emily Dickinson

Meet John Doe

In *Meet John Doe*, a popular movie made by Frank Capra, Gary Cooper played a typical American, an average, undistinguished man whose name nobody knows. John Doe is like Tom, Dick, and Harry, or John Q. Public, a fictitious personage whom lawyers, advertisers, psychiatrists, and sociologists are always summoning up to illustrate a point. But invented though he is, John Doe has an ancient history. In early Roman times, lawyers used such fictitious names to help along a case. Their John Does were called Titus or Gaius if male, or Sempronia or Cornelia if female. Centuries later, British lawyers adopted the most common English male name—John—to play that role. When its legal use became too common and confusing, they added a second name for better identification, such as John-a-land or John-a-farm. John Doe came into use in the 1300s, during the reign of Edward III. The Elizabethans, however, with their flair for color, created legal nicknames that implied social criticism or satire. Contending with John Doe were such imaginary characters as John Makepeace, Henry Woodbegood, and Laurence Lovelittle. Today the name John Doe is still the most frequently used as the fictitious litigant. It is the alias chosen when the name of the party concerned is unknown. (It is Jane Doe when the proceeding involves a woman.) John Doe also provides an identity for real people whose true name is unknown. Someone admitted to a hospital who is unable to identify himself because of his condition is often given that temporary name until he or another can supply the real one. Advertisers have relied on John Doe in their effort to depict the common man their sales messages are designed to reach. Indifferent to the ancient fiction, a real John Doe or Jane Doe appears now and then in the telephone directory.

Rodriguez: Number One

The fastest-growing ethnic group in America are the Hispanics. By the end of the century they may replace Blacks as the country's biggest minority. "Newcomers" they are often called, by people who forget that the Hispanics were the first Europeans to settle in what is now the United States decades before the English came. Rodriguez is now the most common Hispanic name in the country. Following it are Gonzalez, Garcia, Lopez, Rivera, Hernandez, Perez, Sanchez, Torres, and Ortiz. It's likely that sometime in the twenty-first century there may be as many Hispanic names here as English. The complete names of Hispanics generally have three parts: first the given or Christian name, then the middle name, which is the father's name, and last, the mother's name. In alphabetized American directories, the middle or father's name comes first—not the "last name" in the English sense. (Roberto Garcia Perez, for example, would be alphabetized as "Garcia Perez, Roberto," since his father's surname is Garcia and his mother's is Perez, and he would be called Mr. Garcia Perez.) That is, except for those who prefer to be known by their mother's maiden name. The Hispanics, too, have place, occupational, and descriptive names, but patronymics far outnumber the other types.

The Names of Jesus

How many are the names of Jesus? The only names he used for himself in the New Testament are "Son of Man," "Son of God," and "The Son." But Biblical scholars have found fifty-five different designations for Jesus in the New Testament. Among these are Christ, The Lord, He That Cometh, The Bridegroom, The Shepherd, The True Voice, The Lamb, The Firstborn, The Last Adam, and The Beloved.

THE NAME CHASERS

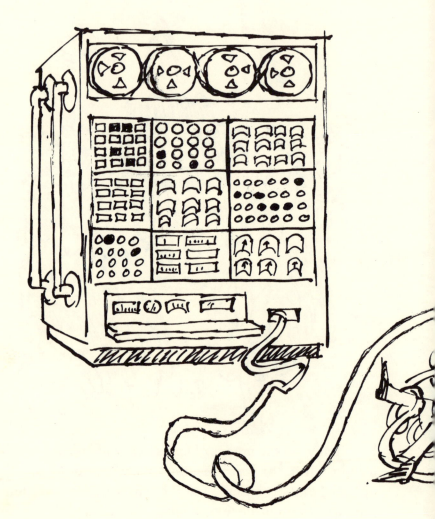

Changing your name in America is a personal right, but there are some agencies that would like to take away that right. Credit bureaus, for instance, would be happy if name changing was impossible; then people who owe money wouldn't slip from reach. The police and the military, too, have an interest in keeping close tabs on people. If everyone had not a name but an individual number their task would be easier. The growth of our computer society helps the name chasers track down their quarry. Every record of one's name is embedded in computers linking each document to every other one. Birth, school, and marriage records; bank accounts, credit reports, and income-tax returns; medical, police, and military records; Social Security and census data—all available now or in the near future to the computer-armed technocrats. Whatever is in a name, for good or bad, will be no secret to them.

NICKNAME

Where does the word "nickname" come from? Once it was "an ekename," that is, "an also-name," meaning one used in place of the regular name. Then it became "a nekename" and finally, "a nickname."

The Nomenclator

How embarrassing it is to meet someone you know but whose name you can't recall! To avoid that awkward moment, the Romans selected a slave with a fine memory, called the nomenclator (name-caller or prompter), to trail along with his master at social functions or while the master was being carried downtown to the Forum in a litter. "Here comes that general you asked a favor of," the nomenclator would whisper, supplying the officer's name. Or "Say hello to Publius Secundus, the ward boss who rounded up the votes for you." When politicians used a name-prompter, Cicero ridiculed them for playing a deception by purchasing a memory. If the statesman did not bother to learn names before election, he asked, would he greet citizens as cordially after the election?

BRENDAN BEGAN IT

Brendan the Navigator (Saint Brendan) was the first white man to see America, and that was in the sixth century, almost a thousand years before Columbus. So goes the claim of many Irish, though they cannot prove it. And among the first to settle—and swiftly be killed—in Jamestown was one "Francis, an Irishman." The flood of Irish immigrants did not commence until the terrible potato famine of the 1840s. Today Irish names sprinkle every directory. Most of them are patronymics. The most common are Murphy (the seafighter), Kelly (the contentious one), Sullivan (the black-eyed one), Ryan (little king), Dun (the brown man), Burke (dweller at the fort), Riley (playful), and O'Brien (hill). The Irish O' means "grandson of" but is often taken as "descendant of." The Fitz in such names as Fitzpatrick or Fitzsimmons means "son of." Mc or Mac are used by Irish and Scots and they, too, mean "son of."

Politicians have always attached great importance to re-membering the names of people they meet. In FDR's time, James A. Farley organized the President's political campaigns. In later years, Farley said proudly that he remembered the names of twenty thousand persons he met while politicking around the country. Twenty-five hundred years before Farley, Cyrus the Great, the Persian king, would call out by memory the names of every officer in his army as he assigned their places and gave them orders. Themistocles, the Greek statesman, is said to have learned the names of all the citizens of Athens. Cicero, too, mastered the names of many of his fellow Romans and wrote how important it was for political leaders to do this: "And now that he was engaging in public life, with greater ardour, he considered it a shameful thing that while craftsmen using vessels that are lifeless, know the name and place and capacity of every one of them, the statesman, on the contrary, whose instruments for carrying out public measures are men, should be indifferent to and careless about knowing his fellow-citizens."

"Consult the Mirror of Names: its hidden meanings are keys to many doors."

—Philo Judaeus

A Dilly

In regions where fundamentalist faiths prevail, the use of pet names in the form of diminutives took hold long ago, to the point where many have been adopted by adults as legal names. One student of naming practices unearthed these examples from the records: Zippie, Sippie, Vandie, Watie, Beadie, Fronzy, Lokie, Mealy, Raffie, Dilly, Sugie, Popsie, Toppie, Ossie, Carlie, Onnie, Nicy, and Bussie.

LUCY STONERS

When the press announced in 1855 that the noted American feminist Lucy Stone would marry Henry Blackwell, the news cheered the enemies of women's rights. They had longed to silence her, and now they hoped her husband would call a halt to her crusade. The Boston *Post* published a poem whose closing lines ran:

> A name like Curtius' shall be his,
> On fame's loud trumpet blown,
> Who with a wedding kiss shuts up
> The mouth of Lucy Stone.

But the poet was wrong. Lucy Stone startled the country by declaring she would keep her birth name (and the marriage made two advocates of women's rights where there had previously been one). "My name," she said, "is the symbol of my identity and must not be lost." Her explanation clashed head on with the common conviction that no married woman could have an individual identity. More and more women followed her example. In 1921 the Lucy Stone League was founded to help women with the legal and other problems involved in keeping their own names after marriage.

NAMELESS

"For all parents fit names to their children as soon as they are born, so that there is no one so poor or so gentle that he is nameless."

—*The Odyssey*

The Foundling

Sir Richard Monday was an English orphan, a foundling who acquired great wealth, which he left to various charities. The poet George Crabbe published these verses in 1807 to describe how such a poor nobody acquired a name:

To name an infant meet our village sires,
Assembled all as such event requires,
Frequent and full, the rural sages sate,
And speakers many urged the long debate,—
Some hardened knaves, who roved the country round,
Had left a babe within the parish bound.—
First, of the fact they questioned—"Was it true?"
The child was brought—"What then remained to do?"
"Was't dead or living?" This was fairly proved;—
'Twas pinched, it roared, and every doubt removed.
Then by what name th' unwelcome guest to call
Was long a question, and it posed them all;
For he who lent it to a babe unknown,
Censorious men might take it for his own:
They looked about, they gravely spoke to all,
And not one *Richard* answered to the call;
Next they inquired the day, when, passing by,
Th' unlucky peasant heard the stranger's cry:
This known,—how food and raiment they might give
Was next debated—for the rogue would live;
At last, with all their words and work content,
Back to their homes the prudent vestry went,
And *Richard Monday* to the workhouse sent.

87

ORDERING the IRISH

The wording of an ancient law decreeing how people should adopt surnames has come down to us from the fifteenth century. By that time the English, who had hereditary surnames, decided that the Irish must have them, too. So in 1465 King Edward IV ordered that every Irishman must not only dress like an Englishmen but should "take to him an English surname of one town such as Sutton, Chester, Trym, Skyrne, Cork, Kinsale: or colour, as whyte, black, brown: or art or science, as smith or carpenter: or office, as cook, butler, and that he and issue shall use this name."

They'd Sooner Fight

They'd sooner fight than make love. Or so you'd think from the tales of the Middle Ages. They seemed to spend untold hours carving one another up. No wonder we have so many military surnames from the days of yore. The fighting forces and their suppliers gave us Archer, Bowman, Bowyer, Stringer, Sword, Arrow, Fletcher (arrow-maker), Armour, Pike (the weapon in this case, not the fish).

The Forgotten Ones

Have you noticed that just about all the occupational names cover work done by males? The work of women was not sent down to us through family names. Women no doubt also acquired occupational nicknames, but since they took their husbands' names upon marriage, it was unlikely that their names would be passed down as the family names. So we have lost some clues to women's role in making the world go round.

HARD WORKERS

The largest single ethnic group in America are the people of German descent. Hard workers by ancient tradition, the Germans brought names that memorialize the work they did from medieval times through their emigration to America. A sample of their surnames: Bauer—farmer, Gerber—leatherworker, Kauffmann—merchant or peddlar, Kramer—shopkeeper, Metzger—butcher, Muller—miller, Schreiner—cabinetmaker, Schultz—carter, Weber—weaver, Zimmermann—carpenter.

Buffalo Bill Kothe

The list of distinguished Americans who once had German names is very long. General John J. Pershing, who commanded American troops in World War I, was the descendant of the immigrant Friederich Pfoersching. The loser in the battle of the Little Big Horn, General George Custer, was the great-grandson of one Köster, a Hessian mercenary of the British, who stayed on in America. The immigrant forefather of President Herbert Hoover was Andreas Huber. Buffalo Bill Cody's true surname was Kothe. Dr. Frederick Cook, the Arctic explorer, was the son of a Koch. George Westinghouse, inventor of the air brake, descended from a Westinghausen. The great-grandfather of novelist Owen Wister was a Wüster. The evangelist Billy Sunday was the son of a Union soldier named Sonntag.

Mr. Later-On

As recently as the 1920s the Persian (now Iranian) government decreed that everyone must have a last name, although up to then people had got along without one. The decree allowed people to choose any name they fancied. Quite a few Mr. Kings, Mr. Emperors, and Mr. Bigs showed up on the new identity cards. Many named themselves after their hometown: Tabrizi, Shirazi, Isfahani (the "i" ending is the possessive). The writer Anne Sinclair Mehdevi reported running across people named Mr. Later-On, Mr. Look-Ahead, Mr. Stand-Up, and Mr. Corpse-Washer. "Such names as these," she said, "were no doubt the gift of the official name-giver, if a man was at a loss to give himself a name."

TOTEM

Among people called "primitive," a system of distinguishing families or clans within the tribe is known as totemism. The totem is a class of living or inanimate objects regarded by these societies as having a blood relationship with the family group. The totem is looked upon as a guardian spirit, and naming follows the totemic system. In Melanesia and throughout Australia, the system of naming is enormously elaborate. Every person bears names of totemic ancestors—birds, stars, spirits, pots—of his or her clan. One individual may have thirty or more such names. In the Wik-Munkan tribe, the fish barramundi is the totem for the men who spear it. The proper names for these men may be: the-barramundi-swims-in-water-and-sees-a-man; the-b.-moves-its-tail-as-it-swims-around-its-eggs; the-b.-breathes; the-b.-has-its-eyes-open; the-b.-breaks-a-spear; the-b.-eats-mullet, et cetera. The women of the tribe whose totem is the crab have such names as: the-crab-has-eggs; tide-takes-crabs-out-to-sea; the-crab-stops-down-hole-and-is-dug-out, and so on.

GUARDIAN

The names that are the special property of a Native American clan are entrusted to a "guardian." Because such lists are often tightly limited, and two people can't hold the same name at the same time, the guardian keeps watch over the available names. His task is to remember the names so that when a child is born he can tell the parents which names are free.

TWINS

Among the Nuer people in Africa, twins are named after birds that fly low, like the guinea fowl. In effect, the Nuer look upon twins as creatures of supernatural origin, like birds. A somewhat similar belief is held by the Kwakiutl Indians of British Columbia. They associate twins with fish. An old man who is himself a twin determines the special characteristics of the infants and according to his diagnosis they are given such names as Silver-Salmon or Sockeye-Salmon. A child born before the birth of twins is later given the name Salmon-Head, while one born after twins is called Salmon-Tail.

WASHINGTON IRVING

Many given names we recognize as quite common were once surnames. The use of surnames as first names began hundreds of years ago in England. When the practice was a novelty, it was confined to "worshipful ancient families." Across the ocean the more democratic Americans began to name their children after heroes of the Revolution. A favorite for male babies was Hancock (after John, the signer) and then Washington. Thousands of sons were named Warren after Joseph Warren's heroic death at Bunker Hill. Then came a flood of christening after Revolutionary idols: Franklin, Jefferson, Otis, Adams, Hamilton, Lafayette. Later it was Madison, Monroe, Jackson, and in the Civil War, Lincoln, Sherman, Grant. During FDR's years in the White House a number of black children were named Roosevelt.

Nameless and Dreamless

When Shakespeare was about forty years old, William Camden published the first important study of personal names by an Englishman. It included this informative and amusing passage about first names among the ancients: "Every person had in the beginning one onely proper name, as among the Jewes, Adam, Joseph, Solomon; among the Aegyptians, Anubis, Amasis, Busiris; among the Chaldaeans, Ninus, Ninias, Semiramis; among the Medians, Astiages, Bardanes, Arbaces; among the Grecians, Diomedes, Ulisses, Orestes; among the Romans, Romulus, Remus, Faustulus; among the old Gaules, Litivacus, Cavarillus, Divitacus; among the Germans, Ariovistus, Arminius, Nassua; among the Britons, Casibellin, Caratac, Calgae; among the ancient English, Hengest, Aella, Kenrie; likewise among all other nations, except the savages of Mount Atlas in Barbary, which were reported to be both namelesse and dreamless."

A Jewish Name?

Is there such a thing as a "Jewish" surname? Students of names ("onomatists") say that it's hard to classify a name as Jewish, for several reasons. Most Sephardic Jews bear Spanish or Portuguese names. Jews of German origin took or were given German names. Many Jews from Eastern Europe carry Slavic names, and those from the Middle East often have the same name as their non-Jewish former countrymen. To add to the difficulty of establishing genuine Jewish names there is the historic fact that a great many Jews have changed their names, and perhaps more than once. Because of all these hurdles, you'd have trouble identifying almost any name as "Jewish." Exceptions are the genuine Hebrew names still in use: Cohen, Ephraim, Halevy, Levi.

2,000 YEARS OLD

Most of the early Chinese immigrants to America came from one province—Kwangtung, on the southeastern coast of China. Unlike many other immigrant groups, the Chinese who settle here seldom change their surnames—perhaps because the Chinese were the first to have hereditary family names, and their names are relatively easy to pronounce. They go back more than two thousand years. Their family names are really clan names in origin, and there are only about sixty different ones. The most common are Chan, Wong, and Lee. Although most keep their surnames, the Chinese usually adopt American given names. But they often change the order of their names, for back home the surnames come first. To avoid confusion here, the names are reversed. Lee Gum Wah, for instance, becomes Gum Wah Lee.

Saints and Angels

The Roman Catholic Church did not have much influence on naming in Western Europe until the 1500s. True, the Church had long asked the faithful to name their offspring after canonized saints or angels. But little attention was paid. Not until the Council of Trent did the Church absolutely oblige its members to use such names in baptism. Then came, in ever greater numbers, Andrew, Barnabas, Bartholomew, James, John, Luke, Mark, Matthew, Michael, Paul, Peter, Philip, Simon. For women it was Agnes, Catherine, Elizabeth, Joan, Margaret, Mary.

NOVELTY

Novelty in names has always had considerable appeal. Back around 1200 in England, the records show such odd ones as Aliena, Celestria, Extranea, Hodierna, Idonea, Ismenia, Melodia, Oriolda, Pharamus, and Splendor. It was mostly girls who were given such splendid tags.

Booze and Bowels

At the time of the American Revolution, hundreds of families had names we find both unusual and funny. We know those names from the Census of 1790. Sample these flavors: Booze, Grog, Pancake, Gravy, Landmiser, Boor, Rascal, Spitter, Pettyfool, Fuss, Flurry, Plump, Daft, Dowdy, Toogood, Lazy, Measles, Bowels, Sinners, Buttery, Dipper, Tubs, Gouge, Dismal, Maggot, Snake, Roach, Hearse, Ghost, Mummy, Fryover, Spitsnoggle, Sydebottom. Some of these names have survived to today. But most people try to shed names that make them appear ridiculous or odd.

PLAYING THE SAX

The names of the famous are often exploited to promote a dish or an article of clothing. We enjoy eating a charlotte russe, a peach Melba, a napoleon, or beef Wellington. Napoleon's conqueror at Waterloo also gave his name to Wellington boots. And what about the Eisenhower jacket and the Mao blouse?

You don't have to be famous to give your name to everyday objects people grow, use, or enjoy. Take Jules Léotard, a French trapeze artist of the nineteenth century. He not only perfected the aerial somersault but also handed down to us the snugly fitting elastic garment—the leotard—worn by aerialists, dancers, and almost everyone else. The gardener William Forsyth gave his name to the forsythia shrub. From Johann Gottfried Zinn, a German botanist, came the zinnia plant. From Sequoyah, the Cherokee who invented his people's alphabet, came the giant evergreen tree, the sequoia, and from Antoine Joseph Sax, the Belgian instrument-maker, came the saxophone.

104

The Ancient Hebrew

In tribal times the ancient Hebrews believed a man's name expressed his personality. Since each person was unique, any one name could apply only to that person. Later, however, the patriarchs clung to a given name and passed it on to the children instead of coining new names. To avoid confusion when only a small number of names were in use, patronymics were adopted—hence Simon Bar-Jonah, meaning "Simon son of Jonah." Hebrew boys were named at circumcision.

TOLSTOY

Russians always have three names—the Christian, the patronymic, and the surname, as in Leo Nikolaevich Tolstoy. When you know a Russian well, you usually address him by the first two. If you ran into Tolstoy on the street you'd call him Leo Nikolaevich. But since the patronymic is honorific, Russians don't use it when signing their name. So the novelist's name appears on his work simply as "Leo Tolstoy." Incidentally, the first Tolstoys who arrived in Russia from the west in 1353 were named Idris. The family name was changed when a Muscovite Grand Prince, Vasily the Blind, gave a favored Idris the affectionate nickname "tolstoy"—"fat."

Bear Facts

Many American Indian societies construct their proper names from the animal identified with their clan. The names mention the name of the animal itself, or they suggest one of its characteristic qualities or habits. Sometimes they refer to some other animal or object with which the clan animal is associated. Osage Indians belonging to the Black Bear clan, for example, have such names as Flashing-eye (of the bear), Tracks-on-prairies, Ground-cleared-of-grass, Black-Bear-woman, and Fat-on-the-skin (of the black bear). Other clan animals to which names are linked include the Bison, Wolf, Turkey, Fish, Fox, and Deer.

The Right Label

Almost no one but her family knows who Margaret Hook-ham is, but all the world recognizes Margot Fonteyn. They are one and the same. When the dancer entered the world of ballet, a more exotic name than her given one was required. So she reshaped Margaret into Margot and worked her mother's name, Fontes, into Fonteyn. Performers in whatever field have long viewed themselves as products that can be more effectively sold to audiences if the right label or trade name is attached. The product name must be pleasing and easily recalled. At a time when religious or ethnic prejudice could hurt a career, actors adopted Anglo-Saxon names to conceal their true identity. Until recently many of the greatest violinists were of Russian-Jewish extraction and the best opera singers were Italian. For a time this led American performers with Anglo-Saxon names to adopt "foreign" names to make themselves more acceptable to audiences.

But not every artist is willing to do that. A change of name is for some too wrenching an experience. They feel they *are* their name and can't abandon it without losing something of themselves, even when their own name may have caused them pain. Jack Lemmon, whose real name that is, had a hard time with it as a child. But he overcame the trouble it caused him, and he refused to give it up when he took to the stage and screen.

It Never Tires Me

In the first edition of Walt Whitman's *Leaves of Grass*, he wrote:

> What am I but a child, pleas'd with the sound of my
>   own name? repeating it over and over;
> I stand apart to hear—it never tires me.

Which Li Wei?

With the population of China so enormous (1,000,000,000 at last report), the authorities have great trouble keeping track of people with the same name. In one district 4,800 women with the same name were recently recorded. In one work unit ten men shared the name Li Wei ("Wei" means "great"). To tell one from another their comrades began calling them "Big Li Wei," "Li Wei No. 2," "Big Eyes Li Wei," "Long-Haired Li Wei," (and so forth). To try to reduce the confusion, one government district is supplying parents with a guide to naming babies.

111

LEGAL NAMES

Is there any such thing as a legal name? The law is cloudy on this point. The Church recognizes only the name given in baptism. Monks and nuns take a new Christian name when they enter an order, and at ordination priests can change their Christian name. It's usually assumed that a person's legal name is the first name given in baptism or registered at birth, plus the surname of the father. In the United States and England, no law limits the parents' choice of a name for a child, but several European countries do regulate naming. An old French law limits names to those known in ancient history or used in religious calendars. German law forbids originating a name: it must be one used before. Americans wishing to drop the old name and take on a new one can do it easily, without applying to a court or government bureau for permission. If they wish to make it a matter of legal record, they simply file an application with a court of record, and the request is usually granted.

SIGNBOARDS

Most people were illiterate in the 1600s and 1700s. Very few streets had names in those days, and if they did, people couldn't read them. Nor could they read names on houses or shops. But they could recognize the colorful signs used for identification. In Central and Eastern Europe, the merchants, the storekeepers, the tavern owners, the artisans became better known by their signboards than by their first names, and soon the sign was taken over as the surname. In the German-speaking countries many family names—non-Jewish as well as Jewish—were acquired in this manner; Adler (eagle), Blum (flower), Engel (angel), Flasche (bottle), Gans (goose), Haas (hare), Krebs (crab), Nussbaum (nut tree), Ochs (steer), Pfau (peacock), Rothschild (red signboard), Schwarzschild (black signboard), Stern (star), Strauss (ostrich), Taub (dove), Einhorn (unicorn), Finkel (finch), Fuchs (fox), Schildkraut (turtle), Stieglitz (goldfinch), Tannenbaum (fir tree), Weinstock (vine), Weintraub (grape), Zissl (sparrow).

PLATO

The children of ancient Greece were given a name on the seventh or tenth day after they were born. The name was the father's choice, and he could change it later if he wished. Children were named after relatives, but rarely after the father. An exception was the orator Demosthenes. With two Demostheneses in town, confusion was avoided by adding to the son's name, "son of Demosthenes of the town of Paiania." Nicknames were common. The real name of the philosopher Plato was Aristocles (after his grandfather). But his gymnastic teacher nicknamed him Plato, meaning "broad," and that name was the one that stuck and became famous.

How can we separate our sense of the self, of who we are, from the name given to us? As the poet Goethe put it, "A man's name is not like a cloak, but like a skin."

Pet names are one kind of nickname. They are the secret names lovers give one another. Ordinary nicknames are public; everyone uses them. But "Puddinlove" or "Dazzlebum" are not names the lovers will reveal to their schoolmates or fellow workers. Such secret names, silly to the outsider, delight the lovers. In Valentine's Day messages run in the London *Times* appear such pet names as Blubs, Cherry Pie, Droobs, Huggles, Snoogles, Woozle, and Zuppy. Take your pick.

TRICKY DICKY

Nicknames are unofficial names, names added to a person's given name. They can be friendly, nasty, or neutral. The hip wriggle that marked Elvis Presley's performances soon had adoring audiences calling him The Pelvis. It was a highly personal nickname, unlike many that are shared by countless people. Take the legions of redheads who become Red, the curly-haired called Curly, the short persons named Shorty. Some criminals, before they are caught and their real names become known, are fixed in the public mind by the nicknames the press gives them. The peculiar murders of Albert DeSalvo, for example, made him feared as the Boston Strangler. Politicians love warm and friendly nicknames, but when they earn unflattering ones (Tricky Dicky Nixon), it can be disastrous.

RAWAUTOAQVAYWOAKY

Very few of the names originally borne by American Indians, or Native Americans, have been kept unchanged. As far back as scholars have been able to go, they have found nothing that could be called fixed surnames. The Indian names in use when whites first arrived proved very difficult for the early colonists to grasp or pronounce. Among the few recorded in the late 1600s were Abozaweramud, Kekroppamont, and Rawautoaqvaywoaky. When Indians were forced onto reservations, the children and adults who entered government schools or hospitals were given American-style names. The Indians' own names were translated, which accounts for the surnames now familiar to us. These names were linked to personal characteristics (Black Eye, Yellow Boy), or to some bird or animal (Fast Horse, Flying Hawk, Red Owl), or to an aspect of the landscape (Red Cedar, Howling Water, High Pine).

For the Birds

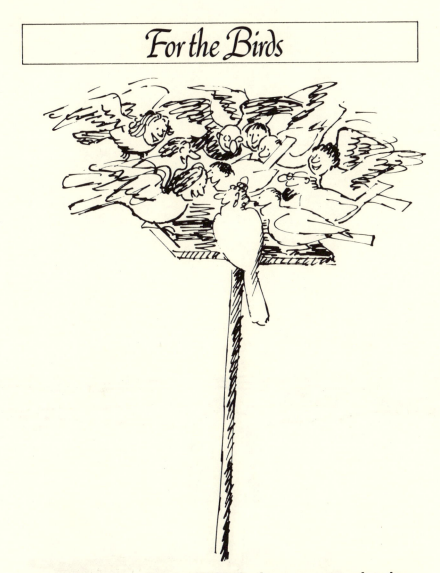

Of family names that recall birds there are enough to keep a bird-feeder busy all day long: Simon *Raven*, Alan *Swallow*, Arthur *Dove*, Florence *Nightingale*, Thomas Love *Peacock*, William *Swan*, James *Crow*, George *Woodcock*, Arnold *Eagle*, Sir Christopher *Wren*, Peter *Finch*, Roi *Partridge*, Peter *Piper*, Richard *Leacock*, Charles *Bulfinch*, James *Larkin*, Calvin *Sparrow*, Lauriston *Thrush*.

A Nameless Sorrow

"The word nameless, especially in poetry and in much prose, signifies an alien, unknown, and almost always unwelcome condition, as when, for instance, a writer speaks of 'a nameless sorrow.' "

—William Saroyan

INTRODUCTION TO APPENDIX

In case you are curious about some of the names referred to in these pages, names you don't recognize, here is brief identification arranged alphabetically. Where you don't find a name listed, it's been plucked from the telephone directory or a work of the imagination. Dates given are for those people no longer living.

Abbott, George. American director, playwright
Armstrong, Louis. American jazz musician (1900–1971)
Bailey, Hilda. American model
Banks, Nathaniel P. American politician and general (1816–1894)
Barber, Samuel. American composer (1910–1981)
Baron, Charles. American law professor
Beard, Charles. American historian (1874–1948)
Black, Hugo. U.S. Supreme Court justice (1886–1971)
Blythe, Ronald. English author
Bright, John. English statesman (1811–1889)
Brook, Alexander. American painter

Bulfinch, Charles. American architect (1763–1844)

Butler, John. American choreographer

Burgess, Anthony. English author

Cardinale, Claudia. Italian actress

Carpenter, Clifford. American actor

Carter, Jimmy. 39th American president

Chamberlain, Neville. British Prime Minister (1869–1940)

Chaplin, Charlie. American film actor, writer, director, producer (1889–1977)

Clerc, Jose-Luis. Argentinian tennis player

Constable, John. British painter (1776–1837)

Dove, Arthur. American painter (1880–1946)

Fiedler, Arthur. American orchestra conductor (1894–1979)

Fields, Joseph. American dramatist (1895–1966)

Finch, Peter. English actor (1916–1977)

Ford, Henry. American car manufacturer (1863–1947)

Forester, Maureen. American singer

Freeman, Orville. U.S. Secretary of Agriculture

Green, Henry. English novelist (1905–1974)

Grove, George. English musicographer (1820–1900)

Hardy, Thomas. English novelist, poet (1840–1928)

Harper, Ida Usted. American suffragist (1851–1931)

Hill, James J. American railroad builder (1838–1916)

Johnson, Samuel. English author (1709–1784)

Juster, Norton. American author

King, Clarence. American geologist (1842–1901)

Knight, Eric. English novelist (1897–1943)

Lake, Veronica. American actress (1919–1973)

Lane, Priscilla. American film actress

Larkin, James. Irish labor leader (1876–1947)

Lincoln, Abraham. 16th U.S. president (1809–1865)

Longfellow, Henry W. American poet (1807–1882)

Marsh, Reginald. American painter (1898–1954)

Mason, George. American statesman (1725–1792)

Meadow, Leon. American writer

Moody, Helen Wills. American tennis champion

Moore, Sam. American wit (1893–1974)

Morris, Wright. American novelist, photographer
Nightingale, Florence. English nurse (1820–1910)
Page, William. American painter (1811–1885)
Painter, George. English biographer
Peacock, Thomas Love. English novelist, poet (1785–1866)
Perkinson, Coleridge Taylor. American composer
Plummer, Christopher. Canadian actor
Poole, Ernest. American novelist (1880–1950)
Pope, Alexander. English poet (1688–1744)
Porter, Andrew. American music critic
Priestley, Joseph. English scientist (1733–1804)
Reeve, Christopher. American actor
Rivers, Thomas M. American bacteriologist (1888–1962)
Saddler, Donald. American choreographer
Short, Bobby. American singer
Speed, Keats. American author
Squire, J. C. English author (1884–1958)
Stewart, Austin. American abolitionist (1799–1865)
Stout, Rex. American novelist (1866–1975)
Swift, Jonathan. English satirist (1667–1745)
Taylor, Elizabeth. American actress
Thatcher, Margaret. British Prime Minister
Thompson, Hunter. American journalist
Tyler, Anne. American novelist
Warden, Jack. American actor
Waters, Ethel. American singer, actress (1900–1977)
Wells, H. G. English author (1866–1946)
White, E. B. American writer
Wilde, Oscar. British dramatist, poet, wit (1845–1900)
Winters, Shelley. American actress
Wise, Stephen S. American reform rabbi (1874–1949)
Wood, Grant. American painter (1892–1942)
Wren, Sir Christopher. English architect (1632–1723)
Wright, Richard. American author (1908–1960)
Young, Andrew. American politician

INDEX

Africa, 29–30, 41, 58–59, 96
adopted names, 33
alias, 39, 73
American names, 31
Anglo-Saxons, 14
animals, 11, 107
appearance, 16–18, 53, 55, 88
artisans, 23
Ashanti, 41, 59
Australia, 94
authors quoted: William Camden, 98; Lewis Carroll, 7; Cicero, 81; George Crabbe, 87; Emily Dickinson, 71; Goethe, 115; Homer, 86; Philo Judaeus, 82; William Saroyan, 120; Elsdon C. Smith, 69; Gertrude Stein, 8; Walt Whitman, 110

Babylon, 33
baseball, 54
biblical names, 33, 36, 66
birds, 119
birth order, 59
Black Muslims, 58

Catholic Church, 101
celebrities, 48
Census of 1790, 103
changing of names, 30, 77, 99, 108
character, 11
charms, 32
China, 8, 13, 100, 111
compulsion, 35

computers, 77
Council of Trent, 101
cyclical change, 36

Delaware, 67
diminutives, 83
Doe, John, 72

Elizabethans, 26, 73, 98
England, 14, 15
entertainers, 22
ethnics, 47

fame, 104
family names. See surnames.
female names, 46, 64–65, 84
first names, 14, 24–26, 59–60, 97
fish, 12
functions, 20

Gentiles, 33
Germany, 70, 91–92, 113
Greece, 114

Hindus, 13
Hispanics, 74

immigrants, 31–34, 36–37, 80
Indians. See Native Americans.
informality, 63
Irish names, 80

Japan, 57
Jesus, 75

Jews, 8, 32-33, 35, 48, 66, 70, 99, 105, 113

kinship, 17, 114
Kwakiutl, 96

landscape, 19
legal names, 112
locality, 17, 19, 88, 93
Lucy Stone League, 84

Melanesia, 94
military names, 89
movie stars, 47

name as property, 14
name guardians, 95
name guide, 111
Native Americans, 8, 11, 31, 67, 95-96, 107, 118
Nazi decrees, 70
nicknames, 16, 27, 40, 53-55, 67, 78, 83, 116-17
nomenclator, 79
Norman Conquest, 15-16
Nuer, 96

occupation, 17, 20-22, 24, 43, 50, 88-91
office, 20-21
onomastics, 8
origins of names: appearance, 16-18, 53, 55, 88; ideas, 14; locality, 17, 19, 88, 93; oc-cupa-tion, 17, 20-22, 24, 43, 50, 88-91; relationship, 17, 114; speech, 15
orphans, 87

patronymics, 35, 74, 80, 105
pen names, 38
performers, 108
Persia, 93
personal description, 18. See also appearance.
personal names. See first names.
personality, 7, 105

pet names. See nicknames.
poets, 52
popularity, 46-47
power, 7, 41, 67
prejudice, 37, 70, 108
protective coloration, 33
Puritans, 27

quantity, 15, 42, 56, 66

recall, 79, 81
regulations, 44, 70, 88, 112
relationship, 17, 114
Revolutionary War heroes, 97
Romans, 13
royalty, 27
Russians, 60, 106

saints' names, 51, 101
Seminole Indians, 11
shapes, 11
shortage of names, 49
sickness, 8, 67
Smithology, 42-43
sorcery, 67
sounds, 8
speech, 15
spelling fashions, 61
Stone, Lucy, League, 84
strange names, 28, 63, 69, 103
suffixes, 35
surnames, 13, 15-17, 24-26, 30, 35, 42-43, 53, 56-57, 62, 66, 97, 99, 103, 113, 118
symbols, 7

taboos, 32
temperament, 11, 16
Tibet, 8
Tiwi, 49
totemism, 94
twins, 96

visionaries, 67

Who's Who, 69
women's names, 64-65, 84